BLACK BOY EYES

IGNORING THE TRUTH
ENSURES A TURBULENT FUTURE.

PALMETTO
PUBLISHING
Charleston, SC
www.PalmettoPublishing.com

Copyright © 2024 by Calvin Lewis

All rights reserved

No portion of this book may be reproduced, stored in a retrieval system, or transmitted in any form by any means–electronic, mechanical, photocopy, recording, or other–except for brief quotations in printed reviews, without prior permission of the author.

Hardcover ISBN: 979-8-8229-5644-5

Paperback ISBN: 979-8-8229-5202-7

BLACK BOY EYES

Anthology of Poems

CALVIN LEWIS

To those who have gone to the light:

    This book is dedicated to my late grandmother, Viola Lewis; to my late earth mother, Rachel S. Davis; to my late sister and her husband, Johnnie Mae and Isaac McDonald; to both of my late brothers, Norman Lewis and Robert Lewis; and to the late Daniel King of London. I miss them and look forward to seeing them in the future.

    Life throws us from A to Z, and we have to endure. Thanks to all of you for the wind that each of you blew beneath my wings. A special and deeper memory for Viola Lewis, the one who taught me that life and death are twin—you can't have one without the other. Know this in your youth, and you won't have a hard time entering the kingdom. Thank you, Grandma.

    Also, a special dedication to my little sis, Felicia "Lil-Bit" Black of Valdosta, Georgia; and also to Linda, Bill, Ross, Keith, Mike, Alex, and Joe Joe Nubin.

Preface

Living Has Become a Problem

Living has become a problem because too many of us want to be someone else other than ourselves. We prefer to chase someone else's dreams and visions instead of developing our own. We are quick to have someone else chase the dreams we cannot achieve ourselves. Yes, just living has become a problem. We are refusing to get to know who we truly are on the inside. We tend to think that we know all the facts about the person we are trying to become, but we know little about who we are ourselves.

We are living in a time when we give no reverence to human capital. Crooked minds do not see straight. God has given men the ability to reason and work things out, yet men refuse to do so. Men do not have to be perfect to work out problems. Men do not need preachers or so-called truth sayers to understand one another. Men must look past the systems we are in and into the hearts of one another. When you give yourself to the system, you lose a part of yourself. We must take a good look at one another and talk about one another's inner truths. God gave all of us an inner light. Do you still have yours? Why not turn it on?

Don't believe the guy who tells you that God told him to tell you what he said. Be careful when you believe in someone who has been on the earth for just a short time and claims to be an expert on what the earth needs. Learn the true history of mankind. Never trust the principal who has a clique. Some people aren't able or capable of giving back anything of what you have given.

Let your love speak for itself. People know how to review your record. I can't see myself looking through someone else's eyes. When all else fails, look inside. I know you see me because I see you. Never work for someone you are afraid of. You could find yourself acting like them and forgetting who you are. Always stay in reality. Just saying.

Table of Contents

Preface	vii
Introduction	1
Child	4
A to Z	5
America, Stop Running Your Children Away	6
Beautiful Lies versus Ugly Truths	7
Come Fly with Me	8
Culture Links (Ode to Nyiieli)	9
To My Beautiful Daughter	10
Empathy	11
England to Me	12
Feeling Free	13
London and Love	14
Rainy Days	15
Face Yourself	16
Fair	17
Fantasy	18
The Beginning Teacher	19
Human to Human	20

If We All Could Right Ourselves, We Could Right the World (Ode to JAH)	22
Joy (Ode to Joy Reid)	24
Live	25
Liars	26
One Ounce of Real Love	27
Time	28
Life Is a Sharp Knife	29
Linda Saunders—My Friend Forever	30
CULTURE MASTER (Ode to Jay-Z)	31
Mr. Superior	34
One Leader	35
One Cannot Predict Life and Love	36
Phone Love	37
Rainy Days with You	39
Running through Life	40
Say Hello to Your Mother Every Day	41
Springtime	42
Stop	43
Plant Your Tree	44
You Are the Hammer	45
Understanding God Is Difficult	46

"Look What We Have Come Through," My Grandmother Would Say	48
Grandma Viola's Democracy	49
Why You So Surprised?	50
Women	51
One Drop	52
Back into My Own	53
The Entity Me	54
Love Is	55
Brown Eyes	56
Forget about It	57
The Best Teacher?	58
Change Starts with You	59
Sparkle Rain	60
Life Is Tough	61
Missing You	62
Marriage	63
Bad Habits	64
Flowers	65
It Is People	66
Be Patient with God	67
Black Boy Eyes	68

Newborn Babies	71
Mental Cages	72
My Love Is Such a Problem to You	73
One Man Rule	74
Love Is the Same for Everybody	75
A True Human Being	76
My Soul Won't Let Me	77
Believe	78
You and Me	79
What Happened to My Dreams?	80
True Friends	81
Death	82
The Age of Deceit and Lies	83
Conclusion	84
About the Author	85

Introduction

Why Poetry?

We are now living in a world where lies and deceit constantly repeat, taking the stage of today. Do what you want to do, say what you want to say, as long as you do it my way. So many men of God, yet so much war. So many years and so many fears. Whatever happened to real tears?

Technology and fantasy seem to be our leaders, and we all know these entities do not believe or bleed. Yet today we allow them to lead. It is man who moves things on this earth we live in. Time is neutral. Time cares not one way or the other about you. You must do the things you need to do and know that every other man is just as important as you. Time will never stop and wait for you. It is not time but man who has brought us to these moments we are living. Yet we refuse to listen to that tiny voice inside all of us.

We have allowed injustice and repression to make themselves at home in all cultures. We allow women to get the brunt of society's sufferings. Evolutionary human growth is looked upon as a joke. Human capital has been overlooked and taken for granted. What's needed now? We need to find out why we are here and what we are here for. We need to listen to that quiet little voice inside each of us, telling us about each other.

The Bible is the most read book ever, they say. Yet it has not stopped the constant bickering among men. Who's God? What's God? What race is God? The book has been excoriated as God's Word. Yet we have moved away from the message it points us to again and again. And the message is each other. We fight hard to stop cultural evolution. Some assume that because others are different, they don't have the right to be here. We need an exegetical study of each other. We are somehow afraid to expand our perspectives by taking a real look inside ourselves, our spiritual selves.

We have misunderstood through time and flawed communications that we are all human. We seem to be afraid of the truth. So generation after generation, we pass these lies down to our youth. We are taught to have delicate sensibilities before we are taught the facts. We are taught to hate the skin others in even though we do not know them. We are taught that when it's someone else other than ourselves, the facts do not matter. We give more reference to the physical and not the spiritual.

When you believe a lie or a delusion, you are damned. Do not let someone teach you to hate. Hate is the beginning of sin. We must truly do unto others as we would have them do unto us. The best way for students to learn is for them to help the teacher teach them and vice versa. Poetry allows us to explore those topics and methods. Poetry opens endless ways to communicate. Poetry points us to our predecessors and our important connection to them. It helps us to know that we do not need to out-sin one another. We just need to love one another.

Poetry is an expression of the unlimited doors in the mind, the experiences of good and bad through neutral time. There have been three waves of history so far—agricultural, industrial, and technological. Yes, we know they all overlap. Those souls that chartered the path before us and carried us through those times must be given reverence truthfully for us to move forward into the next wave. It cannot be done by just one alone.

Mother Nature always gives us directions on how to move to the next wave. One must never give up now for maybe. Denying the truth ensures a turbulent future. Poetry gives you a chance to share your feelings about life experiences that are behind the unlimited doors that we all open and close. It is not physical but spiritual as well that we must discover and express to ourselves and others. We can do this through poetry.

Child

God bless the child.

What world inside God's world have we created?

What road does our posterior take?

Our children are born each day into this same world you and I face.

How do we teach them to face and relate so they may deal with all the confusion and hate they did not create yet must face?

What truthful lessons do we teach and pass on to them?

A to Z

Life throws us from A to Z, and we must endure.

For there is life then death, of this you can be sure.

Day after day we grow, and the older we become, the more we should know.

Yes, life throws us from A to Z, and we must endure.

In this life there are things we can control and things we can't control.

Getting old is one we cannot control.

Life throws us from A to Z, and we must endure.

There will be ups, and there will be downs.

Yes, what goes around comes around.

Life is like a face, sometimes a smile and sometimes a frown.

Life throws us from A to Z, and we must endure.

So live your life as best you can each day,

know that at the end of your endurance, it is death that carries you away.

Life throws us from A to Z, and we must endure.

Yes, we live and endure.

Life then death, of this all can be sure.

America, Stop Running Your Children Away

America, your children are being pushed away.

America, why are you throwing your children away?

America, why are your children being pushed away?

Guns and brawls ignore the law, and your children pay the price.

This one today and that one tomorrow, just like rolling the dice.

America, you are in the eyes of the world, and your examples are beginning to fail.

All nations watch you when the truth you fail to tell.

Your children can now buy bullets as easily as buying nails.

You must treat your youth as human capital by letting them know their lives are not made to spill.

And when they disagree with each other, they don't have to kill.

Teach them that living and becoming wiser is a better deal.

America killing America—is that the blood you want to spill?

America, stop running our children away.

Beautiful Lies versus Ugly Truths

When you disguise bigotry and racism with a beautiful lie,

the only thing that happens is people die.

It's the same old picture again and again,

Nonsense and stupidity between men.

Everyone who's breathing was given life.

God never gave one man life and the other a dice.

God gave all life.

So stop the lie and support the earth.

Learn to love, protect, and understand birth.

We need to grow and learn in our youth that together as a human race,

beautiful lies can never defeat the ugly truths.

Come Fly with Me

Come fly with me, my friend.

We will leave this confusion and travel into truth,

Searching for that resting place where we can set good examples for our youth.

Come fly with me, my friend.

Please reach out and take my hand.

Yes, hand in hand throughout all the earth's land.

Yes, we will search the earth and the universe while spreading love.

Come fly with me.

Culture Links (Ode to Nyiieli)

See the girl with the braids so beautifully laid?

Some call it a new style, but look at her, and you shall see

That this culture has been a part of her all her life.

Some look at her and say she's fine.

I look at her and say to them, "You missed the culture line."

Braids, braids, come in different shades,

From sister to sister, they are made.

So, sister, wear your braids and never care about what anyone thinks

Because you know these are your cultural links.

Braids, braids, so beautifully laid,

They look best on the sister of love.

To My Beautiful Daughter

I want to say something to you that's simple and sweet.

From God in heaven came the day you were born,

So beautiful was this gift I adorned.

A wonderful daughter to us was given.

Through the years as you grew, doing the things daughters do,

I prayed that the Lord would watch over you.

Know this, my daughter, and know it to be true:

I give you all my blessings in all you do.

Always know first, my sweetheart, that Daddy truly loves you.

Empathy

I have needs for my cognitive mind,

But I am not the only one on this ride.

I am always learning, so I take life in stride.

No need to lie, I also have an emotional side.

Life is up and down on my daily ride.

My emotions are shown, and some I choose to hide.

Don't forget, I also have a somatic side.

I recognize and respect spirituality worldwide.

Oh yes, I need understanding from all sides.

England to Me

The island of love and history, mother of discovery.

You are a beautiful place with warm, gentle grace.

Your winters are cold, and your summers are bold, England.

What a pass you have, what a legend you are.

Surviving through time, you continue to grow,

And the lessons learned from various experiences never fail to show.

Mother England, you seem to take living with ease,

And your people seem to be pleased.

Yes, Mother England, I feel your breeze

Blowing to the seas, touching the history that is yours.

Your past and your presence seem to have strength beyond compare.

Yes, England, Mother England, her name and her language
spoken everywhere.

Feeling Free

Do you ever feel free?

Free like a bird to fly.

Free as the heavens and the sky.

Free to have fun and run on the beach under God's sun.

Free to move, free to love someone, expect nothing in return.

Real love can never be hurt.

Free to always tell the truth

And to set good examples for all the youth.

Free to pray or go your own separate way

Without mistakes carrying you astray.

Free to never criticize

And to help those who are less fortunate than you.

For even the more fortunate sometimes need help too.

Feeling free? It's not that hard to do.

Let this frame of mind come from inside of you.

Just live right and tell the truth.

Let this kind of freedom encircle you.

Free. Free. Free.

London and Love

Love is universal.

Love is a summer day in London.

The earth-colored sun covers a special twenty-first-century city of love.

The heath, shining green and gold.

Nature writes her name on all the sights.

Yes, London is love,

Where the Mother Country and nature are sisters.

Rainy Days

As I sit in my room, looking outside my window,

It slowly begins to rain.

For a moment I feel like crying because the rain makes the day seem sad.

Yes, I remember those rainy days in September and the love we had.

Yes, you and I together, holding hands and making plans,

Dreaming of how we would make it better.

Now I sit alone on a rainy day,

Tears running down my face.

The only thing left is traces of memories.

Yes, I remember those rainy days when we would sleep all day.

We had not one care in the world because we were together.

Feeling free, feeling safe, and feeling warm.

Yes, I remember those sweet rainy days in September.

Yes, I still sweetly remember.

Face Yourself

You know when you are right or wrong.

Face yourself.

You know when you are weak or strong.

Face yourself.

Live and let live.

Receive and give the love you seek.

Pass this on to all those you meet.

Stop believing that love calls for retreat.

Understanding love comes to those who seek.

Face yourself and begin to love yourself.

Then you have a chance of loving someone else.

First, you must face yourself.

Fair

Why is it that we all want to be treated fairly

While always asking for much and giving little?

We rush through life and fail to notice the beauty in every human being.

We criticize those who are different from us.

We fight for all the wrong reasons and kill for sport.

We hurt for pleasure.

We have a long way to go and a long way to come.

Why is it that we all want to be treated fairly?

Why is it?

Fantasy

Everything is fake, and nothing is real.

Married to a cell phone and not your skills?

Everything is a fake dog and nothing real.

Yeah, yeah, all fake and nothing real.

Daily you mess around and your life you spill.

Yes, all fake and not real.

Yeah, it's fake, not real.

Do you think you can get through life without any skills?

This way you hurt others with the blood you spill.

Yeah, fake dog, nothing real.

You seem to forget self-control is strength.

Everything is fake, and nothing is real.

Everything is fake, and nothing is real.

It's your life that you truly kill.

You better wake up, dog, and know that you are ruining your life,

And your life is real.

Everything is fake, nothing real.

Yeah, yeah, fake, nothing real.

Ask yourself how many emotions you have spilled.

Living like everything is fake and nothing is real.

The Beginning Teacher

To those teachers just starting,

Know that you are not new.

Remember, it was teachers who taught you,

Both good and bad, I'm sure.

May the good ones be a part of you

So you can do from your heart for your students

What your good teachers did for you.

The truth is in every person, including you.

It must always start with you.

Teach them the things life has taught you.

This is a little message I leave for you.

Teach them how to search for the truth.

Make sure they know that education is not for imitation.

It is for discovery.

Human to Human

I want to ask you something, from one human being to another.

Are you a human who always questions yourself first?

Are you the only human who possesses consciousness?

Do you long to always be free?

Does the truth set you free?

Who is it that tries to enslave you?

Who is it that you try to enslave?

Do you believe that you can encase the human spirit?

What gives you that right?

Is it another human who can set you free?

Do you search for a valid truth?

Have you forgotten that you too were once a youth?

Did you learn to search for reciprocal truth?

Have you gone back and searched to see if you were distorted in your youth?

Are you a human who always questions yourself?

Does everything hateful between men upset you?

Racism and race murder, who introduced you to them?

What's the reasoning behind this?

Is your life based on ignorance or truth?

Does inhuman behavior justify inhuman behavior?

Does racism operate in an illusion?

Does it distort?

What is the truth, and how do you know it to be true?

Are you a human who questions yourself the way you do others?

Answer me, human to human.

If We All Could Right Ourselves, We Could Right the World (Ode to JAH)

To my son, I do not know,

Where do we start, and how do we begin to right this wrong I have done to you?

What topics do we discuss or visit?

How can we communicate?

Is there a way or a chance for us to relate?

When you were an infant, I was that father who let you slip away.

It was only close attention that I had to pay.

Never knew I was making a very serious mistake.

Now you show up forty years later with the emotions and feelings I never felt,

Telling me of the reality you had been dealt.

Now you show up with emotions and feelings I never knew,

Telling me over and over that I abandoned you.

Nothing for me to say or do, for deep down inside, all you say is true.

No room to argue or disagree because what you are saying it's true, you see?

So to my son, I do not know,

How do I get to know you?

We cannot play father-and-son games.

I can go on forever telling you I feel deeply ashamed.

But it was your heart, son, that searched out your name.

Not for show, not for fame.

You just wanted to know your real family and your real name.

The pain I feel inside can never be fully expressed to you.

But I shall attempt to bear this pain and hope you know what I ask of you is true.

Is there a way for me to truly get to know you?

To my son, I do not know.

Is there a way for me to love you?

To the son I do not know,

Is there a way for us to grow?

Tell me from here where do we go?

To the son I do not know.

Joy (Ode to Joy Reid)

Dreams of joy are always a part of my life,

So many things happening along the way.

The ups and downs from day to day.

I must be truthful in the things I say

Because so many truthful things can be twisted these days.

Joy is always in my heart and life,

So I try to live with joy.

The bridges of joy are many.

To burn those bridges would be silly.

What happens when you want to return home?

Dreams of happiness and joy are always in my heart,

Born into a world that seems torn apart.

My drive and my push come from the love in my heart.

The worldwide community from which we all are a part must be held together by an intelligent heart.

Yes, dreams of having love and peace are always in my heart,

And my life I try to live with joy.

So turn your telescope around and look at me through the correct end.

Dreams of happiness have always resided in my heart and in my life,

So I try to live my life with joy.

Live

When we live, we have so many years

To shed so many tears and fight so many fears.

Then we leave after so many years.

During this time, when we were in each other's space,

I truly hope I made my space a better place for you to stand.

Liars

Beware of the liar.

They will destroy you.

Beware of the liar.

They may come at any time.

Beware of the liar.

They may fool you again.

Beware of the liar,

They are carriers of sin.

Yes, this is the jigsaw puzzle that confuses many men.

Yes, a liar is always at the root of our sins.

Beware of the liar.

One Ounce of Real Love

Just an ounce of real love is bound to make you feel better,

Something real for a change, something different from the game people play,

Something honest and strong.

We, as people, have been on the planet for a long time,

Yet we still struggle with the simple art of loving.

Just an ounce of real love is bound to make you feel better.

Could it be that we have hurt one another so much and played so many games

That true love no longer exists?

Or could it be that when we differ, we fail to let understanding persist?

Or is it just something about love we don't realize exists?

Just an ounce of real love is bound to make you feel better.

Yes, just a simple ounce.

Yes, real love is what we all should be looking for.

Just an ounce will do.

Time

Time is neutral and always with us.

Let us hold hands and run into time.

Let us kiss and fuse into each other's minds.

Let us smile and reflect on each other's souls.

Let us create a love that's never been told.

Let us walk and begin to run,

Giving, loving, and having fun.

Let us learn how to give and receive.

Let us all find our place under God's sun.

Let us hold hands and run into time.

Life Is a Sharp Knife

All the great religions claim to favor life,

Yet the entire world is full of strife.

People are cut down daily, like butter through a sharp knife.

What is it that we see?

We see more and more that hate is simply not what we were created for.

Yet we have ultimate issues with love for each other.

We need to stop, analyze, and realize that we need to make a change.

We all must visualize a world for a better life.

We must stop living on the psychological blades of a sharp knife.

Linda Saunders—My Friend Forever

Lights up those around her.

Independent.

Noble thinker.

Dauntless darling.

Affectionate mother.

Sagacity.

Adoration.

Uncommon and unadulterated.

Natural human being.

Dreamer of truth.

Eloquent and effective.

Righteous.

Saintly.

My friend, here is how I begin to say thank you again and again.

All we say and do mean nothing if we fail to have humility for each other.

Love to a great friend and a great mother.

I treasure the love we have for each other.

CULTURE MASTER (Ode to Jay-Z)

Woke up this morning still trying to understand and find the many things I'm after.

Made me realize I am a culture master.

I can get along with any culture that rejects man-made disasters.

Yes, one must be a culture master.

Never start fights or cut down any culture.

Never walk around bragging about how much better I am than you.

Never smear things out of your mouth unless you know them to be true.

Always try very hard to set good examples for the youth.

Yes, all the youth never focus on just the ethnic group they belong to.

Yes, yes, I am a culture master.

I can get along with the roughest and the toughest.

Have genuine respect for the soft and the hard.

Don't mind them coming to my property, if they respect my yard.

Yes, yes, now you can see what I am after.

Culture master—always giving your culture the same respect, my culture is after.

Citizen of the universe. Yes, my brother is a culture master.

Can you see what I am after?

Must be able to get along with all cultures without causing all man-made disasters.

Yo-yo, just know I'm a culture of the master.

What's that? Culture master.

Come on. Come on. Deep down. Deep down.

The same love and respect we all are after.

Yes, culture master.

I am living and loving my life without causing any other men any disasters.

Yes, culture master.

Culture master, do you hear what I say?

Culture master, I do not consider myself to be better or more than any other,

And I am no dearer to myself than another is to himself.

I only have so many years to live, full of tears and fears.

Don't want to use words of disaster.

The same love your culture is after,

It's the same love my culture is after.

Lifelong culture masters always help us prevent man-made disasters.

Yes, culture master, love, peace, laughter, and knowing each other's culture helps free us from self-assertive aggression.

You know what I'm talking about.

Man created disaster.

Lies that bring no understanding.

Do the things you know are proper to man and his well-being. All men.

Yeah, yeah, culture Master, can't you see what my heart is after?

Every day in every way.

Culture master.

Mr. Superior

When you formulate by asserting your own justice, setting yourself up as a law by which to judge another because he believes and looks different from you. This kills mercy in one's heart. I am still learning and discovering the need for love and how to live. When you claim to be God's best friend but refuse to introduce him to me, you become suspect. I feel insulted to be called ignorant by a dear friend because I feel he is wrong from my point of view. What's your real name? Your conversation is very judgmental. You are doing to me what you ask me not to do to you. You are trying to tell me that you know how much I love myself. You seem to think that your baseless assumptions are preordained. My life and my experiences rest upon my ability to take myself and those I love seriously. When it comes to the Lord I choose to worship, the consequences will be mine. Misery loves company. You can never give me wisdom with a fragile ego. If your road map was so true, how come you go through the same things I go through? You seem to think that life was only given to you. Mr. Superior, nothing is true for you. You think life was meant for just you. Look around and you will see, that could never be true.

One Leader

No one leader is needed.

We all need to lead as soon as we are old enough.

We need to do it with deliberate speed.

We all need to work on peace.

We all need to respect the things humans need.

When we understand this, all our loads are lighter.

It helps us realize there's plenty on the earth for the needy.

We run into our problems trying to satisfy the greedy.

We do not need one leader.

One Cannot Predict Life and Love

You cannot predict life and love.

We never know what all our days are made of.

You cannot predict life and love.

Everyone goes through stress and strife

And enters this adventure called life a blank sheet of paper.

Life writes its experiences on us all.

You see, these things that life writes on us are full of despair and fairness.

Some are good and some are mean; some are seen and some are unseen.

You cannot predict life and love.

So whether you're eight or eighty, blind, sick, healthy, rich, silly, or crazy, life makes its mark on you.

No matter the race, no matter the place, you cannot predict life and love.

No matter the person, life writes *down* what you *record*.

Phone Love

Our children are now in love with cell phones.

Even though you're sitting right there beside them, without that phone, they still feel alone.

No human interaction do they feel they need.

Your silence on the matter worsens it with deliberate speed.

Cell phone computer love,

This is what they think they need.

You must let them know that no matter how much time they spend on technology,

It can never replace human love.

You will always find that the phone and technology have no emotional content.

They can't love you back.

Give your children some of yourself.

Though you may not have much time.

Do the best that you can do.

You know, the way your family did it with you.

Talk, smile, communicate, emotionally relate, face-to-face,

The way humans should do.

If we don't do this, we will find new mental illnesses beginning to exist.

Do not sit and give our children away to technology.

My sisters and brothers, teach your children that human capital is what they should Druther.

No phone or technology can ever love you like your father, mother, sister, or brother.

No matter how much technology time spent, it will never have emotional content.

Rainy Days with You

Rainy days are for dreams.

They seem so sad, it seems.

No sight of the sun.

Misty day, rainy day, dreamy day.

Things seem so sad.

No place for fast fun to be had.

Yes, rainy days are out for my dreams.

Watching the rainbow as it extends its beams.

Not a care in the world.

I am in a dream, it seems.

I always enjoy these beautiful moments with you.

Rainy days are meant for you and me.

Running through Life

Running through life,

Moving too fast.

Do you think this life will always last,

Moving into the future, not learning from your past?

Don't you know there's no place else to go except where we all must go?

No matter how you run, no matter where you hide, you have to take this ride.

Slow down and walk through life so you can see the reflections that are produced by you.

Say Hello to Your Mother Every Day

Say hello to your mother every day.
Even if it's just once a week, that's OK.
Mother—oh, true fruit of the motherland.
You are wondrous and full of miracles.
Your love is everlasting.
From you I am, and from I you are.
Through love and time, we have learned to be friends.
Yes, through real love, we are one, and we know it.
Through time, we have adapted many ways to survive.
Some are good and some are bad, yet we have survived.
You are the mother, the ancient rock.
Our destiny is the same.
You are the true fruit, and I live in you before I even know myself.
You are a wonder of nature.
You are the mother, and I love you.
May you shine throughout the universe,
And may all of us whom your pains have procured always respect and understand you.
So say hello to your mother every day.
Even once a week is better than nothing; that can pass as OK.
Yes, you are mother, mom, nana, muh-dear, memaw, and I love you.
Say hello to your mother every day.

Springtime

Mother Nature and beauty are sisters.

They're beautiful together.

Make the birds sing.

This is a true sign of spring.

Love seems to be in the air.

Time moves on without a care.

New life comes up from all around.

A man helps by putting a seed in the ground.

People everywhere seem to move without care,

Enjoying the sun and putting away their despair.

Yes, it is springtime,

When nature seems to wake up from her cold sleep

And gently beautifies the world like a baby sheep.

All the creatures of the world are happy and gay,

Yes, my friend, that's the secret of the new spring day.

Stop

Stop lying to God, and things will work out.

Stop talking about loving one another and start doing it.

Not just where you live and dwell but on the earth.

Stop lying to God, and things will work out.

Stop lying about how superior you are to all of God's creations.

In his eyes we are all special.

If we just stop lying to God, we will all see that he loves you just as much as he loves me.

Stop lying to God, and you shall see that things will work out.

When men lie to and about each other, it creates an indefatigable amount of doubt.

Just stop lying to God, and things will work out.

Stop.

Plant Your Tree

If it is all bad that you see, maybe you need to replant your tree.

For every woman and every man, sometimes you must change your plan and take a stronger stand.

When dealing with the fact that life comes to us through no fault of our own,

We need to check ourselves and see what we have grown.

If it is all bad that you see, maybe you need to replant your tree.

When you find your life divided against itself, you must plant in new soil.

When you are in the middle of a great change, that is when you must rearrange.

If it is all bad that you see, maybe you need to replant your tree.

You Are the Hammer

You are the hammer that drives my nail into your love.

That deep love that I never get enough of.

You are the hammer, and your strike is as soft as cotton.

Your aim is always straight, and your rhythm is part of the air I breathe.

You are the hammer that drives my nail into your love.

That special love that only you can give.

You are that hammer with the strike that is soft as cotton,

That drives a nail so deep in my heart that it can never be forgotten.

Yes, you are that special hammer.

Understanding God Is Difficult

A true understanding of God is very difficult.

One must have faith to navigate the road to join him.

A lot of good and bad along the way.

It will test your faith from day to day.

Listen carefully to what your preachers say.

But never ignore what the God inside of you say.

Remember, a true understanding of God is difficult.

So many experts, yet when we look at the world,

We find lots of talk and no action.

We allow injustice and repression to make themselves at home in our church and cultures.

We watch what people do to one another.

How quickly life falls apart when men lose sight of the experiences God has already shown them.

Humans suffer from their own human-to-human mistreatment.

Men tell men who is worthy of life.

None of them truly understand how this all began.

Yes, the man tells the man who is worthy of life.

Race murder we have come to witness.

Mothers, fathers, grandmothers alike are given no reverence.

Is it Satan or men who are responsible?

We are in a fight to save humanity from humanity.

All lives need to protect life.

We will always need to know what we were to become better at what we are.

We must always confront the truth that God made all of us.

Understanding God is difficult because men want to fight human evolution.

When we fight human evolution, it sets us back.

God's plans will carry themselves out no matter what we do.

It does not matter if we like them or not.

As difficult as God's plans seem to be, it is man you must keep your eyes on.

Man believes that by destroying the truth, he will find a solution.

Yes, understanding God is very difficult to understand.

If we could just get past some of man's pollution, we could find our much-needed solution. Understanding God, it's difficult.

Somehow, we stop trying to understand God and started trying to be God.

"Look What We Have Come Through," My Grandmother Would Say

Look at all we have come through just to know a little about ourselves.

Do you truly believe the earth was created for just you alone?

Love all and see where it takes us.

Hate all and see what it makes us.

Do you really think the earth was made for you alone?

Do not love people for their color.

The hate you see in one is also in the other.

Do you really think the earth was made for just you alone?

It is the same earth we all must travel through.

The issue is what and where it is we are trying to get to.

Is it bigger than me and you?

Please, I need to know for sure.

Do you really think this earth was made for just you alone?

Grandma Viola's Democracy

From the beginning, as a little boy, I knew there was something special about the word "democracy." I could tell from the look and joy on my grandmother's face when the subject matter was discussed. Although she could not read or write, she understood the implications. The watery tears in her eyes were not the same tears she got when she was hurt and cried from sadness, but instead, they came from a good joy came from inside.

Democracy—to her, it offered freedom. One man, one vote, the fundamental law of the land, and most of all, freedom for all women and for all men. "I pledge allegiance to the flag," she would say, "of the United States of America and to the republic for which it stands, one nation under God, indivisible, and with liberty and justice for all." She believed this came from God. This great country had kept the call, even though remnants of Jim Crow still existed. "It will be OK someday," she would say. "We are maturing," she insisted.

As a little black boy, I absorbed those feelings and beliefs. "I was born in America, the same as anyone else born here in America," she would say. "You are an American. Of this dirt of which you were born. Men are not imprisoned by God but by men. All souls yearn for freedom." Not once would she cry a racial word. "Tell the truth, son, and stay away from lies," she would say. "Because in this country, we have issues with practicing what we preach. You must feel what it is to be an American and learn to reflect that in your actions toward all people." Yes, one nation under God. America's truly a nation that God must teach. That's why God has the reins.

Why You So Surprised?

Why are you so surprised when they tell you lies? Why?

Are you so surprised when they claim to be so wise?

When now in their cries they are using Jesus as the prize?

Why won't you see what your eyes visualize?

Can you not see how they use Jesus in their lies,

covering sins and at the same time plotting your demise?

Tell me, sister, tell me, brother, why are you so surprised?

Yeah, the same old lies without vision.

They ignore human cries and chase the skies,

Worshipping the same old wrongful lies.

God has already made it clear that all must die and return to him.

Now ask yourself why the same old lies.

Why are you so surprised?

Same old reasons to keep taking people's lives.

Why are you so surprised?

It is not a disguise.

Look closely.

It is right before your eyes.

Women

Women, the future is yours.

Take a trip back through time.

Life is evolving and growing inside.

Not just pain the woman feels in her quest to be equal, but truth.

The kind that is sincere.

The kind that does not fear.

Look around you.

She is the pain taker who bore you here.

The stress she has and the love she carries throughout day-to-day strife,

Yet she never stops giving life.

So, men, take a good look at her.

Stop playing your games.

She is a part of you.

She is your life.

Look at her.

She could someday be your mother, sister, grandmother, or daughter that you meet in life.

She could become your evolving wife.

Her future is yours.

Women are the perfect example of human love sent from God above.

One Drop

Like a single drop of water, I am dropped into the ocean of life,

Not knowing the rivers, lakes, ponds, and seas I am now a part of.

Does my drop make a difference?

What can I, just one single drop, learn from all these bodies of water?

To learn this, I must take the journey.

When taking the journey, I gain experience about my connections and curiosities.

Now I begin to experience the different bodies of water.

This gives me a wider recognition of myself and experiences.

The purpose of my learning has been to expose me to the different bodies I am connected to.

To know when to take the low and when to take the high tides becomes a necessity.

Do not see what you are learning as a means to an end.

See it as a world of discovery.

Go and discover what your one drop can do.

You can never fail if your one drop is done with love.

One drop.

Back into My Own

I'm so glad I'm back on my own,

So glad I've learned to be strong from the experiences I've had in my life.

Yes, I've ran around and played games.

Some folks say I've even gained fame.

Yet I never knew me until I looked into the mirror and began to see the inner being within.

Self-knowledge is your light in the world.

When you discover it, it will let you shine like a beautiful pearl.

The Entity Me

That entity me.

It has all the characteristics you have.

You have flesh just like me.

The true difference is simply our minds.

Love Is

A universal feeling is love.

Love is the unending rock to lean on.

Love is God.

Love is all that is good and all that represents the truth.

Love is an expression of feelings that can't be touched.

Love is something that we all need to learn how to express.

Learning to love each other is man's biggest test.

Love is.

True love teaches us that we were all created by the same Creator.

Brown Eyes

Your brown eyes are like brown sugar.

They are deep and rich like honey.

Brown eyes I love to see,

Especially when you look at me.

Brown-eyed girl, go on and smile.

Just let me stare into them just for a little while.

Brown-eyed girl, I like your style.

You have the type of eyes that drive guys wild.

They make me think you came from your own style.

Yes, you're that brown-eyed girl I met somewhere in time and space.

I've never met a girl with brown eyes as beautiful as yours.

Brown-eyed girl, won't you look and smile at me?

Forget about It

Forget about the days when it's been cloudy,

But don't forget about your hours in the sun.

Forget about the times when you have been defeated,

But don't forget about your victories.

Forget about the times when you have been lonely,

But don't forget the precious moments you spent with that one and only.

Forget about the mistakes that you have made,

But don't forget about your lessons learned.

Forget about plans that didn't work out right,

But never forget your right to live and your right to get better.

The Best Teacher?

Life is the best teacher.

It helps us get to know ourselves.

Only I can master me,

And only you can master you.

But life is the master of us all,

So know yourself.

See what you have to be proud of

When you are being graded by the best teacher.

Take a good look at your life.

Change Starts with You

I need to change.

I need to reject these dreadful habits.

I need to show discipline.

Oh, how I need to change.

Oh, how I want to get better.

That's it, start something new.

Oh, I guess I'll do it tomorrow.

I need to change.

Sparkle Rain

Sparkle like the mist in Africa.
Sweet like the kiss in the spring.
To you rain this song I sing.
You fall without a care
And when you come to me,
It seems you're everywhere.
Yes, water, cool water, godsent water.
From the sky you got your birth,
But the real reason you come is to clean God's earth.
Rain. Rain. Rain.
Sparkle rain.

Life Is Tough

Life is so tough.

I feel I've had enough.

Sometimes I feel like giving up.

Things come down on me.

Falling heavy in the dark night.

My dream seems so far away.

I want to run from it all.

Yet my inner divine self keeps my head up.

Knowing my history helps me.

I want to live and try to understand the roads of life.

They are all different to each of us yet the same.

Those who want to destroy themselves have not learned the meaning of life and its substance. There are many treasures that God has given us.

Life is the greatest of them all.

Many have not learned to simply love themselves.

They take their own lives because they have not learned to accept the imperfections in others and in themselves.

Live and learn to understand your inner self.

The thought of death should make you evaluate life. Your own…

Missing You

Honey, I miss you so much.

That sweet feeling you bring with your gentle touch.

It is so hard without you, and I miss you very much.

The strength that you have shown me has never let me down.

The love you give me is true and sound.

I need and miss your company, and I need it now.

Your company is something real.

It is something one should never spill.

Yes, my friend, my love, I miss you and wish you were here.

Your love is not made of words but something deeper.

Yes, I am missing you,

For you have taught me that love is not a deal but a sacrifice.

Missing you.

Marriage

Two as one and one as two.

If you don't mean it, it's something you should not do.

It's teamwork both day and night,

And the same applies when you're out of each other's sight.

It's not a game, and it won't bring you fame,

So to get married and not mean it is a damn shame.

Your respect for each other must be real and not some blame game.

Bad Habits

The worst problem one can have is bad habits.

They can control our minds and ruin our lives.

Make us hurt those we love most.

Make us feel like we are being controlled by a ghost.

Bad habits are not jokes.

They can lead to heart attacks or strokes.

Bad habits are problems that face all folks.

Flowers

Colors of love and times you show.

And when the winter comes in, you must go,

Not to escape but to revive only on another day.

You are the flowers of the earth,

And your beauty transcends from year to year.

Through all this time, I have never seen the flower shed a single tear.

I love you now and forever, beautiful flower, because you know your reality and your reasons for being here.

It Is People

IT IS PEOPLE, NOT COLOR, THAT DISCRIMINATES

Be Patient with God

When I learned to be patient with God, it helped me grow.

All that time I was being impatient with myself, thinking it was God who was not being patient with me.

It taught me how to get up and do.

It taught me movement to the truth.

God favors movement.

Being patient with God opened my innermost creativity.

I learned that for every wrong we create, we cleave to God for spiritual assistance when we are in existential peril.

I am very grateful to God for allowing me to be patient with him.

And in doing so, I have learned to see most trouble coming my way.

I have learned that most of my sins can be handled by me.

I learned that we must confront the lie, accept the truth, and be patient with God.

This is the most beautiful patience I've ever known.

It allows me some understanding about how the spirit moves.

This is the most beautiful patience I've ever known.

Black Boy Eyes

Born into this world of preconceived notions that have already judged me guilty before I take a breath.

No matter how honest I am, I have been judged guilty.

No matter how clean I am, the world has somehow been taught to see me as filthy.

My life can be taken for nothing at all, and no one is found guilty.

Yes, born into a world of preconceived notions that have already found me guilty.

Black boy, black boy, how come there are no reasons given about why there is this open season on you?

You are murdered for going out for a jog or simply eating a burger in your car.

This is why your mother is always saying, "Son, don't go far."

It does not seem to matter where but who you are.

You are shot for innocently knocking on the wrong door.

Beat then have your head pressed onto the floor.

This does not happen to other boys.

This is an event you are known for.

Is it a ploy, or is it designed to target the black boy?

Black boy, born into a world of preconceived notions that have already judged you as guilty.

Therefore, black boy, you must recognize your life as your own.

Be familiar and at home with yourself.

Never express this kind of ignorance toward anyone else.

Always carry intelligent ways to protect yourself.

Yes, as you go into this world of preconceived notions that do not allow you to define yourself authentically,

You must learn how to live and protect yourself.

Always be aware of this preconceived notion, and remember, it spreads across all lands and all oceans.

You must always confront this preconceived notion that you are guilty for being born.

You must know and understand your history.

You must know that God did not create this man-made mystery.

Black boy, black boy, going into a world where life is experiences and experiences are relationships.

Know that relationships are not in isolation.

So protect yourself with intelligent action.

Black boy, born into this world to live your life as God intended.

Live and try to avoid the ignorance.

Be an example of righteous dignity.

Black boy, be proud of who you are.

Black boy, born into this world that you must see through black boy eyes.

Newborn Babies

What will we make of them?

Boys and girls are born every second into this world.

They have no say in the matter.

Among us they come.

What do we tell them?

Where do they truly come from?

How do they learn to hate and love one another?

How do they know who is Black or White?

How do they know what is wrong or right?

How do they know which is the right fight?

Who teaches them to distinguish day from night and darkness from light?

Is it not us who model their plight?

Mental Cages

Blood is not always family, and family is not always blood.

Our lives are like blank pages that we write on during its many stages.

We must free our five senses from the psychological self-made mental cages.

Love is the key to the many pages that we go through throughout the ages.

Can you find yourself in yourself?

Blood is not always family, and family is not always blood.

My Love Is Such a Problem to You

Why is my love such a problem to you?

You call me names and bring me shame just for wanting to love you.

Are you punishing yourself through me?

Why is my love such a problem to you?

I have done nothing to you other than remain true.

Yet you seem happy when you make me blue.

What is it that I did to you?

I gave you my word that in this relationship I would love only you.

I told you my love is priceless,

So why is my love such a problem to you?

Is it because to thine self you are not true?

Is it because you are not true, so you think others are just like you?

One Man Rule

CAN ONE MAN NEUTER A COUNTRY

Love Is the Same for Everybody

Love is a power that you cannot neglect.

It is a power you must respect.

When it is around, you can always detect the feeling it reflects.

Love demands genuine respect.

It takes nothing.

It is a neutral phenomenon.

Love is something you must give but may not get back in return.

True love is given to you without demands.

Love is not a fantasy or a symbolic gesture.

It is genuine.

Love cannot be manipulated or overstipulated.

When it is truly love, you don't have to prove your worth or your value.

Love is a power that you cannot neglect.

A True Human Being

Who and what defines a true human being?

How does a true human being see the world we live in?

A true human being belongs to the human family.

Does a true human being have unlimited passion?

Does a true human being live to destroy others?

Does a true human being believe that life transcends race?

Does life connect us all?

Does a true human being face life and death?

Ask yourself, are you a true human being?

My Soul Won't Let Me

You keep telling me I am inferior to you, but my soul will not accept that lie. The unending attack on God's highest creation does not make sense. You seem to be upset at the way God created his world. You seek an arbitrary end and conclusion to his highest creations. You are busy trying to decide the fate of others when fate does not discriminate. You try to simplify death, and you try to control it. You think that you have won because you kill the flesh. Sin and death are the best of friends in your eyes. Your attitude has become contaminated. You think the world end has no ambiguity. You make life less real with your righteous assumptions based on false facts. You feel this way because you are afraid of your own death. I won't tell you that you are inferior to me because your soul is like my soul, and it will not accept that lie. You can never shake my fidelity because love must be a true goal for all men. It's the only thing that can transform our true lives. It can save us from our ignorance of one another. We must respect one another's integrity. Some may believe your lies, but my soul won't let me.

Believe

So many things I never believed until it happened. Experience gives self-strength and wisdom. One needs to silence the mind occasionally. Meditate. You live in ignorance when you avoid or ignore the facts. I sit here and look deeply into myself, trying to reach the gateway to my soul. This journey I have been on from the days of my youth through the days when I am old. Like tossing me from times of hot and times of cold. This flesh only lasts a while, and then the soul returns to God's light. So many things I never believed until they happened. All my life I have been engaged with many men who mouth off the words of the scripture but who do not understand them or try to practice them in life. It is the kind of life I have tried to live that helped me see the reflections of his will. So many things I never believed until they happened to me through him.

You and Me

Easy nights and mellow days are what I like best.

Give me my sweetheart and a quiet night, and you can keep the rest.

I don't need no money, and I don't need no car.

You see, none of these things made us what we are.

Only time and patience with lots of goodwill are the reasons we are together still.

So if you are like me and you want to be real,

Just tell her how much you love her and stick to the deal.

Easy nights and mellow days are what I like best.

Give me my sweetheart, and you can keep the rest.

What Happened to My Dreams?

I put my dreams on hold because I wanted to see how far you and I could go.

Instead of hurting me the way you did, all you had to say was "I don't want you anymore."

But you played me, and it hurt me so much.

Now I look at you, and I can't stand to have your touch.

You made me lose my feelings and my desire for you.

Yes, I put my dreams on hold just to see how far you and I could go.

I look and feel, but I cannot find that feeling anymore.

What happened to my dreams?

The new ones I wanted to dream with you do not work, it seems.

So I am glad I can go back and visit my old dreams.

We all must start over at times, it seems.

What happened to my dreams?

True Friends

The best friends one can have are true friends.

There is no friend like a real friend.

They will stick by your side until the very end.

They demand no payment for being your friend.

They never take the credit for keeping the friendship together.

Positive friendship lasts forever.

The nature of all real friendship is sincerity.

The relationship is based on respect.

No false pretending.

Just being your real self.

Never distorting or falsifying anything about the relationship.

No fake friendship to be mine.

Lord knows true friends are hard to find.

I am very blessed because it is hard to find one true friend in an entire lifetime.

True friends.

Death

Death is everyone's fate.

We do not ask for or demand this life we are given.

In life we are driven toward death from the very start.

We are not taught to respect death until it affects us.

Ignorance of death makes us ignorant of life.

We only have two paths in life: to live and then to die.

We do not have to visit any church or join any group to look inside ourselves.

Going to someone for the answer won't help.

We must understand death and how it fits into our lives.

We build and we transform from day to day and year to year.

We have one life with many stages.

Knowing ourselves through these stages is a foundation we can build on.

The more we know ourselves, the more we can grow.

When we have seen all these stages and experienced all the life pages and can do no more,

We will find death at the door, no matter how early or late.

This is every human being's fate.

Be sure to teach your children how life and death relates.

The Age of Deceit and Lies

Over and over our history repeats all the things we thought had met defeat. We face an unending process of learning. We have somehow ignored our practice sessions for learning to love. We search everywhere for love and ignore the fact that we are the key to nature. We may argue until doomsday about deceit and lies. We completely ignore the mother who cries. We insist on feeding ourselves lies. Yet we suffer when we cut human ties. We are the ones who created this deceit and a world full of lies.

This is the age we are living in. We have lost sight of mercy that heals in every way. Words can be deceptive, but history will always hold the truth. At no time can the mystery of life be true if we have decided to lie to ourselves. If we become obsessed with lying to ourselves, we will not leave enough space for love. We become as cold as the machine. Deceit and lies seem to be the ways in which man carries out his deceptions. We all must draw from the wisdom that life itself teaches us.

Modern man has become very disillusioned with this technological wave he has created. Yet in the deepest places in our hearts, let's not let technological despair fill up the void. We must not be deceived into believing all the deceit and lies being thrown at us. We must always remember that when it comes to man, there is nothing new. We must simply figure out how to love each other and know our reasons for being here. Love is our true destination. Life at its best comes when we respect and love one another. We must not overlook the heart and mind. Over and over our history repeats all the things we thought had met defeat.

Conclusion

Poetry gives us endless expressions. It can free our minds from delusions. It can help us get closer and have a better understanding of one another. Poetry is universal. It allows thoughtful men and women to be heard and understood. It helps us see God in every moment of our lives. It shows us that material pleasure is only temporary. It leads us to a mature consciousness. It shows us how to commit ourselves to action. It reflects our integrity. It shows us that a wise conscience is one that is willing to respect all other consciousness. It shows us that love is a special way of living. It teaches us that humans have moral conflicts. It teaches us that life is not static but an unfolding experience. It shows us that each human must come to grips with his own individuality. It expresses differences between a good life and a bad life. It shows us that we all must search for our full potential and recognize the same in others. It shows us that we must respect and recognize the integrity in one another. It shows us that our actions at times do not reflect our own self-interest. It helps us seek love and not perfection. It teaches us how to love and forgive. The truths in poetry are indefatigable.

About the Author

Calvin Lewis was born in Valdosta, Georgia, and raised in Riviera Beach, Florida. He has been called a Fla-Ga boy his whole life. This is his first book, a compilation of poems he has written over his lifetime.

In this book he shares poems and expressions seen through the eyes he has been looking through. He believes that life throws us from A to Z and that we must endure. *Black Boy Eyes* is an expression of himself, reflecting the world he has observed. It contains no oral processes of avocation, only experiences he has endured in life and expresses from the heart.

www.ingramcontent.com/pod-product-compliance
Lightning Source LLC
LaVergne TN
LVHW092056060526
838201LV00047B/1413